Profiles in American History

The Life and Times of

STEPHEN F. AUSTIN

Mitchell Lane
PUBLISHERS

P.O. Box 196 · Hockessin, Delaware 19707

Titles in the Series

The Life and Times of

STEPHEN F. AUSTIN

Russell Roberts

Printing   1   2   3   4   5   6   7   8   9

Library of Congress Cataloging-in-Publication Data
Roberts, Russell, 1953–
   The life and times of Stephen F. Austin / by Russell Roberts.
      p. cm. — (Profiles in American history)
   Includes bibliographical references and index.
   Audience: Grades 7-8.
   ISBN 978-1-58415-531-7 (library bound)
   1. Austin, Stephen F. (Stephen Fuller), 1793–1836—Juvenile literature.
2. Pioneers—Texas—Biography—Juvenile literature. 3. Texas—History—Revolution, 1835–1836—Juvenile literature. 4. Texas—History—To 1846—Juvenile literature.
5. Frontier and pioneer life—Texas—Juvenile literature.
I. Title.
F389.A942R63 2008
976.4'03092—dc22
[B]
                                                                          2007000792

ABOUT THE AUTHOR: Russell Roberts has written and published nearly 40 books for adults and children on a variety of subjects, including baseball, memory power, business, New Jersey history, Texas history, and travel. The lives of American figures of distinction is a particular area of interest for him. He has written numerous books for Mitchell Lane Publishers, including *Nathaniel Hawthorne, Thomas Jefferson, Holidays and Celebrations in Colonial America, Daniel Boone,* and *The Lost Continent of Atlantis.* He lives in Bordentown, New Jersey, with his family and a fat, fuzzy, and crafty calico cat named Rusti.

PHOTO CREDITS: Cover—North Wind Picture Archives; pp. 3, 10, 27, 29—Center for American History, The University of Texas; p. 12—Valerie Holifield/GFDL; p. 15—Karl Bodmer; p. 18—Sfajacks/GFDL; p. 40—Texas State Library and Archives Commission; p. 41—Library of Congress, pp. 34, 42—Antonio Rafael de la Cova/Latin American Studies.

PUBLISHER'S NOTE: This story is based on the author's extensive research, which he believes to be accurate. Documentation of such research is contained on page 47.

   The internet sites referenced herein were active as of the publication date. Due to the fleeting nature of some web sites, we cannot guarantee they will all be active when you are reading this book.

                                                                          PLB

Profiles in American History

Contents

*For Your Information

Stephen F. Austin, painted with a gun and what may be a hunting dog. In truth, Austin was neither a hunter nor a military man. His lack of military skill would greatly affect his later life.

CHAPTER 1

Imprisoned

Stephen Austin sat alone in cell #15 in a prison in Mexico City, with nothing to do but stare at the stone walls. A few weeks earlier, on January 3, 1834, Austin had been arrested on his way back to the Texas town of San Felipe de Austin—a town that ironically had been named in his honor by the Mexican authorities.

Austin was a well-known figure in Texas and Mexico—the first and best-known Texas empresario. He remembered how he hadn't even wanted to go to Texas at first. It had been his father, Moses Austin, who had dreamed of going to Texas and starting life all over again, leaving behind the debts he had accumulated in Missouri and starting anew. In Texas, Moses was going to rescue the Austin name.

But Moses had died before he had a chance to put his plans into motion, so it had fallen to Stephen to carry them forward. It was Stephen, also strangled by debt, who decided to pick up where his father had left off, make his fortune in Texas, and restore the Austin family's good name.

Now he sat in a Mexican prison, his dreams in tatters. He thought he had been a friend of the Mexican government. Even while the Texas air was filled with talk of revolution against Mexico, he had preached patience and loyalty. Mexico had asked him and the families who'd followed him to be loyal to it; Austin had steadfastly honored that request.

Austin had come to Mexico City to present a petition asking that Texas, which was part of the Mexican state of Coahuila y Texas, become its own state. Antonio López de Santa Anna, the Mexican leader, had seemed sympathetic to Texas. But now Austin was in prison.

His jail cell was dirty, dingy, and reeked with foul odors. The only feeble light came from a filthy skylight high up in the roof. He wasn't allowed books, or to socialize with other prisoners; his only conversation with someone from the outside came with the occasional visit from his lawyer. He shared food with a mouse, which had become trusting enough to let him pet it. His only other companions were the spiders, ants, and other insects that crawled around his cell as he watched. Otherwise, he did nothing all day but stare at the walls in his sixteen-by-thirteen-foot cell.

Weeks and months passed. The wheels of the Mexican legal system ground glacially forward. No court seemed to have jurisdiction over Austin's case, which bounced from one court to another. Eventually the conditions of his imprisonment were softened—he was given books, allowed to socialize with other inmates, and moved to less odious jails—but he was still a captive.

Day after day went by, with no hope, no chance that maybe tomorrow he would finally be able to answer the charges against him. Austin knew that Mexico's legal system allowed the government to keep a person jailed while it collected evidence. He knew that he could be in prison a very long time.

As time went on, Austin became more and more depressed. He was forty years old, of slight build, with a lined face. He was prematurely losing his hair. His reserved demeanor masked the fire he felt inside for Texas—and his outrage over being jailed.

His health was poor. The food was bad. The air inside the prison was foul and filled with disease. How much longer could he hold out? What did the future hold? Did he even have a future?

"I expect," he wrote, "to die in this prison."[1]

Santa Anna

Remembered primarily as the Mexican general who slaughtered the Alamo defenders, Antonio López de Santa Anna was probably the most prominent figure in Mexican politics and military affairs in the nineteenth century. Unfortunately, however, he did little to help his country build a strong democratic government.

Santa Anna was born in the Mexican state of Vera Cruz in 1794. At age sixteen, when Mexico was still under Spanish rule, he joined the army. For a while Santa Anna battled Mexican revolutionaries who were fighting Spain for independence. In 1821 he switched to the revolutionary side, and helped bring about the defeat of Spain. Two years later he was again fighting the existing government, only this time it was the Mexican government that he had helped install.

In 1829 his popularity soared when he successfully defended Mexico against an attempt by Spain to reclaim the country. He was elected president of Mexico in 1833. However, what began as a seemingly enlightened and liberal rule became more despotic as Santa Anna assumed more and more power for himself.

In 1836 he led an invasion force of Mexican troops to crush the independence movement in Texas. He overwhelmed the Alamo defenders on March 6, but was himself defeated and taken prisoner by Sam Houston's Texas Army at the Battle of San Jacinto in April. The victory assured Texas of its independence.

Santa Anna (with red shawl) surrendered to Sam Houston (lying down) after losing the Battle of San Jacinto

Returning to Mexico, Santa Anna was forced from power. However, in 1838 he defeated a French invasion attempt, regained popularity, and by 1841 was once again a dictatorial president. He was overthrown two years later, and was discredited when the Americans defeated Mexico in the Mexican-American War of 1846–1848. Nevertheless, he once again became president in 1853 and established yet another brutal regime.

Santa Anna was finally overthrown for good in 1855; he never again returned to power. He died in 1876.

Austin as a young man. He had been a failure at all the ventures he tried in life until he picked up his dead father's dream to settle Texas.

CHAPTER 2

Early Life

The Austin family were Puritans who had first arrived in America in the 1630s from the southern part of England. They settled in Massachusetts. Moses Austin, Stephen's father, was born in 1761. When he was old enough, Moses went to Philadelphia to assist his brother Stephen as a tailor and merchant. In 1784 Moses went to Richmond, Virginia, to open his own business. He returned to Philadelphia the following year to marry Mary "Maria" Brown.

In 1788 Moses's brother Stephen came to Virginia. He and Moses took over the operation of a lead mine in Wythe County, Virginia, approximately 250 miles from Richmond. A village named Austinville grew up around the mine.

In Austinville on November 3, 1793, Stephen Fuller Austin was born to Moses and Maria. He was the first Austin child to survive past a year old; two previous children, both daughters, had died before reaching their first birthday. A sister named Emily soon joined Stephen.

Stephen had fond memories of his early childhood. Before long, however, happiness became more elusive because of the increasing financial burden of the mine and its operation. Thus Moses was more than ready to move on when he heard about large amounts of lead deposits in the Spanish province of Upper Louisiana (later to

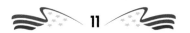

become Missouri). After going there and scouting it out (he masqueraded as an important leader in order to impress Spanish officials), Moses and his entire family, as well as about forty other relatives and workers, left Virginia on June 8, 1798, for Missouri.

It was a hard trip. Three of Stephen's relatives died, and others in the group either died from illness or got separated. When they landed at Kaskaskia, Missouri, only two people could walk ashore from their ship without assistance.

The Austin family settled in St. Genevieve, the village closest to a place called Mine à Breton, which held significant lead deposits. Moses built an elegant house for his family called Durham Hall. He also opened a store. Young Stephen played with Native American children from the nearby Kickapoo tribe.

In 1803 Stephen's brother, James Elijah Brown (known as Brown), was born. The population of Mine à Breton was mixed among French, Spanish, American, African-American, and Native American peoples. This helped Stephen develop a tolerance for and understanding of other nationalities and cultures.

In 1804 Stephen was sent to school at Bacon Academy in Connecticut. His courses included English, math, geometry, geography, and natural philosophy. The school was very strict, prohibiting such things as loud talking and whistling. Even so, Stephen participated in his share of schoolboy pranks, such as helping to place a coffin on the teacher's chair.

The Austin family home in St. Genevieve. The family traveled there from Virginia on a terribly difficult trip. Not everyone survived it.

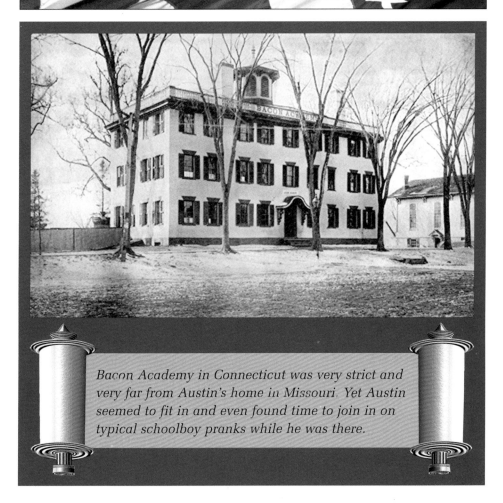

Bacon Academy in Connecticut was very strict and very far from Austin's home in Missouri. Yet Austin seemed to fit in and even found time to join in on typical schoolboy pranks while he was there.

After graduating from Bacon Academy at the end of 1807, Moses decided that Stephen would attend Transylvania University in Lexington, Kentucky. There, Stephen studied math, history, geography, and philosophy. He also was very interested in girls. One in particular was named Eliza, but Stephen left Transylvania before anything could develop between them. (Eliza wound up marrying Stephen's classmate Robert Todd. They had a daughter named Mary, who would someday wed a man from Illinois named Abraham Lincoln.)

Austin enjoyed participating in Lexington's social activities, particularly dancing. Yet he was forced to leave school in April 1810, when he was 16½ years old, to return home to Missouri. Moses was

preparing to make a business trip to the East Coast, and he needed Stephen to look after things in his absence.

Moses left shortly after Stephen arrived in Mine à Breton. Although lead was not selling well, and finances in the Austin household were tight, Stephen managed to keep everything running.

Having proven himself capable, Stephen was ready for Moses's next assignment. In mid-1811, Maria went east to visit friends. Moses was unable to give her much money for the trip, and by late autumn her funds were running low. Moses decided to send Stephen down the Mississippi River to New Orleans on a barge filled with lead and other goods. He was supposed to conduct some business in New Orleans, then sail to New York, where he was to sell the lead and give the money to his mother, who was meeting him there.

However, numerous incidents, including Stephen's illness from malaria, delayed the trip until the spring of 1812. Finally, around the second week of May, Stephen set sail upon the Mississippi.

The trip was difficult. A massive earthquake had struck the area of New Madrid, Missouri, in December 1811, making the river more unpredictable than ever. Sandbars and small waterfalls had formed where none had been before, and Austin had to be extremely careful.

Finally, about 60 miles north of New Orleans, the barge hit a sandbar and sank in 10 feet of water. Unable to recover any of the cargo until the water level in the river dropped, Austin continued to New Orleans. Once there, he learned that the United States had declared war against Great Britain. The War of 1812 had begun.

The war brought business to a halt in New Orleans. Although he successfully recovered the lead cargo from his sunken barge, Stephen tried for months but was unable to sell it.

There was a great danger that the Sac and Fox Native American tribes, who were friendly with the British, would attack American settlements in Missouri. On May 24, 1813, Stephen Austin became an ensign in the Missouri militia. On September 1, the day after his sister Emily's wedding, Stephen left for a campaign against the Native Americans. The campaign ended one month later without any significant battles.

During the War of 1812, Missouri residents were worried that they would be attacked by the Sac and Fox tribes, which were friendly with the British. Austin joined the militia but didn't see any significant action.

By the time Stephen arrived back at Mine à Breton in October 1813, his father's financial problems had become even greater. People began suing Moses to obtain the money he owed them. Finally, in the autumn of 1816, Moses decided to lease the mines to Stephen and move with Maria to the town of Herculaneum, Missouri.

Stephen won a seat in the territorial legislature of Missouri in late 1815. There he worked on numerous issues that would help his district, such as better roads, mail service, and land ownership.

By late 1818, Stephen Austin seemed to be a successful businessman, legislator, and civic leader. But looks can be deceiving. In reality his business was not doing well, and debts were mounting

for the entire Austin family. That New Year's Eve, Stephen made a solemn vow: "When the day arrives that the whole family are out of Debt, I mean to celibrate [sic] it as my wedding day—which will never come untill [sic] then."[1] What he meant was that he would not get married or try to start his own life and career until his family was out of debt. To accomplish his goal, he looked to the west.

What Austin saw was what many other Americans at this time saw: vast expanses of open land to the west. For a man who felt that his life had reached a dead end in his present situation, the idea of escaping the mistakes of the past and beginning all over again was a powerful temptation. Many people left their homes and headed west, hoping for a fresh start.

In April 1819, Stephen Austin became one of those people. He set his sights on an area called Long Prairie, on the Red River in what is today southwestern Arkansas. His plan was simple: He intended to establish land claims in Arkansas in places that he thought would someday become towns or highways. Then when the town or road was being planned, the land would be very valuable. Austin also established a farm and store in Long Prairie.

But the optimism of spring soon turned into the disappointment of autumn. The store and farm did not make much money. Most of his land claims did not do well either. It was not surprising that Austin expressed unhappiness at his situation. His gloom was further magnified by bad health. When he considered his situation along with his father's, Stephen's depression grew even worse. Both he and his father owed a lot of money. Going back to Missouri was not possible because of all his debts there, yet when he had tried to set up a new life in Arkansas, that too became a failure. The Austins' troubles seemed to have the proud family surrounded.

But Moses Austin thought he saw a way out . . . in Texas.

New Madrid Earthquakes

The New Madrid earthquakes that struck Missouri in the winter of 1811–1812 were some of the most powerful in the history of the United States. The quakes, which numbered three in all, and their aftershocks caused damage as far away as Charlestown, South Carolina. The earthquakes even caused church bells to ring in Boston, Massachusetts—nearly 1,000 miles away.

It is estimated that the three quakes would have registered 8.0 on the not-yet-invented Richter scale. (The Richter scale measures earthquake intensity. The higher

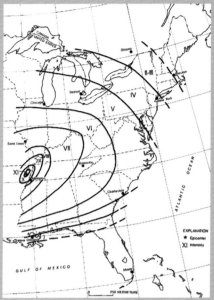

The New Madrid earthquake of December 16, 1811

the number, the more severe the earthquake, with 8.5 being "devastating.")

The first quake hit on December 16, 1811. It was centered around the town of New Madrid, in the southeastern corner of Missouri near the Mississippi River. The quake began in early morning, when it was still dark, with a deafening roar. According to an eyewitness account, the vibrations knocked everyone out of bed. All anyone could hear were the screams of people and animals. People were tossed around like dolls, and blood from injuries was everywhere.

The second quake struck on January 23, 1812. Reports are that it was as bad as or worse than the first one. Many people thought the quakes were announcing the end of the world. The third quake hit on February 8. Severe aftershocks rattled the region for months.

According to eyewitness accounts, the earth cracked open, the ground rolled in a wavelike motion, and pieces of land rose or sank, or rose then sank. The quakes also changed the face of the mighty Mississippi River. For example, a steamboat captain who had moored to an island in the river for the night awoke to find that the island had disappeared beneath the waters.

A statue of Stephen Austin at Stephen F. Austin State University in Nacogdoches, Texas. The base of the statue is a star, which represents the state of Texas.

CHAPTER
3

Gone to Texas

Late in 1820, with fifty dollars he had borrowed, Moses Austin departed for Texas and the town of San Antonio de Béxar, which is today San Antonio, Texas. The territory was part of Mexico.

Mexico at that time was under the rule of Spain, but Spain was not a powerful nation anymore, and it had trouble ruling a country an ocean away. Several revolutions, some led by Americans and some by Mexicans, had erupted against the Spanish, but they still clung to Mexico.

Meanwhile, there was little development in Texas. Spanish government officials realized that more settlement was needed. They didn't want other countries and people to settle the land, claim it as their own, and cause trouble for Spain. This was particularly true of Americans: Spanish officials had watched Americans spread westward—"like oil on a cloth"[1]—in increasing numbers, and knew it was just a matter of time until Texas was choked with Americans.

Moses planned to play on these fears by telling the Spanish that if they gave him permission to bring families into Texas, these families would become loyal Spanish citizens. For Moses personally, the Texas venture was a new start and a way to regain some wealth.

The trip did not begin well. At their first meeting, the Texas governor ordered Moses out of Texas immediately. As Moses dejectedly walked back through the San Antonio streets, he met Baron

de Bastrop, an old friend who knew the governor. Bastrop talked to him, who now received Moses's idea enthusiastically and said he would recommend its acceptance. Back in the United States, Moses got word in mid-May, 1821, that the Spanish had approved his idea.

"A new chance presents itself,"[2] he said jubilantly. But it was not to be. He had pushed himself too hard. On June 10, 1821, Moses Austin died.

Meanwhile, Stephen had drifted to New Orleans to seek his own new start. There he became friends with lawyer Joseph H. Hawkins. Hawkins gave Austin a job in his law office, let him live in his home, and gave him money to buy food to send to his mother and sister back home. Hawkins also let Austin use his law books to study to become a lawyer.

By this time Austin had grown into a slender young man, about five feet nine inches tall, with dark hair, hazel eyes, and fair skin that easily sunburned. Thanks to Hawkins's kindness, he seemed finally to be on a path that would provide him with a steady income, thus allowing him to pay off his debts and perhaps help his family. Although he was concerned about his father's safety on his Texas trip, Stephen had no intention of participating.

History has long portrayed Austin's participation in the Texas scheme as a case of the dutiful son following his father's dying wishes. In a letter, Stephen's mother, Maria, told him how his dying father "called me to his bed side and with much distress and difficulty of speech, begged me to tell you to take his place."[3]

However, what Moses Austin did before he died also swayed Stephen's decision. Moses had written to Hawkins about the Texas venture and promised him a joint interest in it. Hawkins was enthusiastic about the idea, and offered to pay for the return expedition to Mexico. Hawkins's influence and financial involvement almost certainly pushed Stephen to get involved in the Texas scheme before he even knew of his father's death. Stephen started for Texas to meet with a group that Moses had put together on June 21, 1821—nine days before he received word of his father's death.

On July 1, 1821, Stephen wrote a letter advertising that his father had received permission to bring 300 American families to Texas.

This letter, which appeared in newspapers as far away as Kentucky, invited families to sign up for the adventure.

On July 16, Austin and a group of fourteen others crossed the Sabine River and entered Texas on their way to San Antonio. As they traveled across Texas, east to west, the landscape changed. Scrubby pine trees and bushes were replaced by healthy oak, hickory, and pecan trees; the soil changed from dry and sandy to rich and dark: good for farming. Buffalo, deer, and bear were everywhere. Wild grapevines edged the rivers. Austin had been concerned that the land might not be able to support people, but now his concerns vanished.

When the group reached San Antonio on August 12, they were met with amazing news: Mexico had won its independence from Spain. Fortunately, local officials determined that the change in leadership would not affect the land grant: Each family would get 320 acres of farmland near a river, and 640 acres of grazing land. In addition, a wife would receive 200 acres, each child 100 acres, and each slave 50 acres. Thus a family with just one child would receive almost two square miles of land.

Austin left San Antonio to explore Texas and decide where he wanted his land grant. As he traveled through the Texas countryside, all doubts about the venture quickly disappeared. He later wrote: "The idea of contributing to fill it [Texas] with a civilized and industrious population filled my soul with enthusiasm."[4]

Arriving back in Natchitoches, Louisiana, in October, Austin found almost 100 letters from people eager to relocate to Texas. More letters were undoubtedly waiting for him in New Orleans and other places. His advertisements had gained more attention than he realized.

It seemed as if Austin was well on his way to wiping out both his own and his family's debts. He hoped to be named an overseer of American immigration into Mexico by Mexican authorities, and to be able to collect a fee for granting them land. When Austin calculated the amount of money he hoped to make that way, it came to nearly $50,000—an enormous sum for that time.

But that was in the future. Right then, Austin still had to borrow money to finance the first group of families settling in Mexico. With funds borrowed from Hawkins and elsewhere, he bought a small

schooner called the *Lively* and filled it with food, tools, and other things the settlers would need. He sent the ship ahead, telling the crew to anchor at the mouth of the Colorado River and wait for him. Then, in mid-December, Austin set out again for Texas.

Texas was in a depressed condition at this time. Its population of Tejanos (Mexicans living in Texas) had sunk to about 2,500. They lived mostly in two towns: San Antonio and Goliad. A third town, Nacogdoches, had once been thriving but was now nearly abandoned. The Louisiana Purchase had placed land-hungry Americans right on the Texas border. Mexico knew that Americans would never be able to resist all that open space. Speculation about Texas expansion was the topic of conversation among many Americans. So, like Spain, Mexico hoped that by populating Texas legally with families loyal to Mexico, it could prevent American expansion into the region (or squatting, as it was called).

One person who arrived early on in Texas was Brown Austin, Stephen's brother. Stephen had not seen his brother for several years. Brown quickly became someone that Stephen trusted and relied upon for advice.

Stephen would need all the friends he could have. He was never able to find the *Lively*, which blew off course and eventually went back to the United States. Without those critical supplies, the first months for the new colonists were hard. They survived on turkey and deer meat. Medicine was nonexistent. Austin raced about, trying to help the colonists as much as he could.

Then, on a trip to San Antonio to report on his progress, Austin was met with devastating news. The new central government in Mexico City had decided that Austin had no authority to distribute land or do anything else associated with the settlers. Indeed, it was possible that he did not even have permission to establish an American colony in Texas.

Quickly Austin prepared to go to Mexico City and personally plead his case to the Mexican authorities. Was his dream of a new start in Texas about to end before it even got started?

The Revolt of Miguel Hidalgo y Costilla

Mexico made several attempts to break away from Spain before finally becoming independent in 1821. One of the most famous revolts was lead by Miguel Hidalgo y Costilla (right) in 1810.

Born in 1753, Hidalgo became an ordained priest in 1778. In 1803 he was put in charge of the parish in the town of Dolores. Hidalgo quickly stamped himself as an enemy of the *gachupines* (native Spaniards), who had been oppressing the Mexicans for centuries. Trying to improve their economic condition, he taught the Mexicans how to plant crops, such as olives, mulberries, and grapes. He also showed them how to manufacture pottery and leather goods.

All of this angered the *gachupines*, who planned to arrest Hidalgo. Warned ahead of time, Hidalgo made a spur-of-the-moment decision on September 16, 1810. He called for the arrest of the town's *gachupines* and proclaimed a revolutionary crusade to free Mexico of the Spanish. He carried with him a picture depicting the Virgin of Guadalupe, the patron saint of Mexico. This became the symbol of the revolution.

Mexicans, long under the boot heels of the *gachupines*, flocked to his cause, and Hidalgo's army swelled in number to as many as 60,000. The army was undisciplined, however. In the battle for the city of Guanajuato, they massacred government forces and engaged in an excess of death and destruction.

Hidalgo was upset by the class warfare he had unleashed. As his army approached Mexico City, heavy casualties and desertions caused his numbers to dwindle. Afraid of how his army would act, Hidalgo abandoned plans to enter Mexico City. Even more desertions followed. Finally, on January 11, 1811, Hidalgo's remaining forces were soundly beaten by government troops. The rebellion was over. Hidalgo fled north, but was captured and executed by the Spanish. However, his name and memory live on. The state of Hidalgo was named after him, and the town of Dolores was renamed Dolores Hidalgo. September 16 is celebrated in Mexico as Independence Day.

For Your Information

Emperor Agustín de Iturbide delayed and delayed on Austin's plans for Texas's colonization. Then, after finally signing the colonization bill, de Iturbide abdicated, and Austin was back at square one.

CHAPTER
4

The Empresario

The political situation in Mexico was boiling with uncertainty when Austin arrived there in late April, 1822. Austin had hoped to be away from his colony in Texas for only a few weeks, because he knew that his presence there was critical for helping the settlers get organized. But the unsettled state of Mexican affairs continually frustrated him. The Mexican Congress had been working on an overall colonization law, and the political climate slowed their progress.

While Austin waited, he did what he could to advance his cause. He learned Spanish and made contacts with government officials. Always he stressed his loyalty to Mexico. He also met other men who were seeking permission to establish colonies in Texas.

The normally slow legislative process was reduced to a crawl by the volatile political situation. Contralists (those who wanted a strong central government) and Federalists (those who wanted to give the states, like Texas, more power) were battling for political supremacy.

Even when progress seemed imminent, it was not. In August 1822, the Mexican Congress finally received the first colonization bill from the committee. They sent it back to the committee for revision. Then nineteen congressional members were arrested for treason. All political business came to a near standstill for the next several

months. The colonization bill crawled through congress. Then the Mexican emperor, Agustín de Iturbide, dissolved the Mexican congress on October 31. A smaller version of congress, called the *Junta Nacional Instituyente*, was created. They drafted a new colonization bill. There was nothing Austin could do but have patience throughout all these delays. "Blessed is he that holdeth out to the end," he wrote, "and I am determined to persevere."[1]

What complicated matters for Austin was that he needed two separate matters decided. One was to have an overall colonization bill approved so that the Mexican government would have guidelines to grant settlers land. Then he needed his specific land grant request approved. The second could not occur without the first.

In late November 1822, the junta finally sent a colonization bill to the emperor. Austin was optimistic—until a revolution against Iturbide broke out, delaying matters once again. Iturbide finally signed the colonization bill in early January. Once again Austin felt hopeful—and once again his hopes were dashed. Austin's specific plans languished for two more months. To revive them, he turned to some of the many important and powerful political friends in the Mexican government he had made while waiting.

It turned out to be a good thing that he did so. Iturbide abdicated on March 19, 1823. The new Mexican congress then canceled all laws passed under his regime. Thus the new colonization law for which Austin had waited so long was invalidated.

But the new government was more liberal than the previous one, and on April 11, they rewarded Austin's patience. Instead of the 640 acres he had sought for them, each colonist would receive a *league* (4,428 acres, for ranching) and a *labor* (177 acres, for farming). Austin himself was given 100,000 acres, and he was permitted to charge settlers 12½ cents per acre for surveying and other expenses. Furthermore, no taxes would be charged on Texas settlers for six years. The Mexicans required only that the settlers be Roman Catholic and that they become Mexican citizens. Even here, however, the Mexicans agreed not to enforce the Catholic requirement. Although it had taken almost one year to accomplish something that Austin had hoped he could do in a few weeks, the waiting had been well worth it.

Austin giving land to one of the first families to settle in Texas. Many people, eager for a fresh start, answered Austin's call for settler families.

When Austin rode out of Mexico City on April 18, 1823, he had become the first Texas empresario—someone who signed a contract with the Mexican government to bring settlers into Texas. Although other empresarios would later be approved, Austin was the first.

Austin's long absence from his colony had hurt his cause. Word filtered back to the United States that he had died. Other reports detailed the hardships facing those in Texas from a combination of hostile Native Americans, bandits, poor weather, and crop failures. American newspapers in western territories prominently featured such stories. These territories were competing with Texas for settlers, so any bad news about Texas was good news for them.

Once Austin returned to the colony in early August, 1823, he immediately started to set things right. He issued land grants to 272 families, and 25 more soon followed. These families became known in Texas lore as the Old Three Hundred. In 1824, a town capital was established on the Brazos River called San Felipe de Austin. It was the first Anglo-American colony in Texas.

Austin also dealt with the nearby Native Americans. There were four tribes in the area—the Karankawas, Tonkawas, Wacos, and Tawakonis—and with them Austin used a mixture of negotiation, patience, reward, and force. He was always very aware that the Native Americans could force the colonists to leave Texas by making life miserable, so he was careful not to engage in all-out warfare with them.

Since there were no Mexican officials in the area, Austin had to establish a governmental system. He had to be careful there too: The Mexican government was watching to make sure that he established a government faithful to Mexico, but the Americans in the colony valued their independence and would rebel at a government that was too strict. Austin had to walk a fine line to meet the expectations of both groups.

The empresario system was designed to regulate the settlement of Texas, and assure that only the desirable—Catholic families loyal to Mexico—were admitted. Initially it worked as it was intended. Austin set stringent requirements for members of his colony: Each family head had to produce written documents attesting to his good character, industry, and sobriety. Those who were idle or drank too much were forced out. The colony was so peaceful that most left their doors unlatched.

Men enjoyed the benefits of Texas—its freedom from government officials, its wide-open spaces, and the chance to start fresh—but most women were not so lucky. There was little for women to do in Texas, and many talked sadly about the lives and friends they had left behind. The settlers' cabins were bare and sparse. It was hard to grow a garden, and there was no cloth or cotton to spin or weave, no churches to attend, no schools to get kids ready for—in effect, nothing for them to do. As one woman said: "Texas was a hell for women."[2]

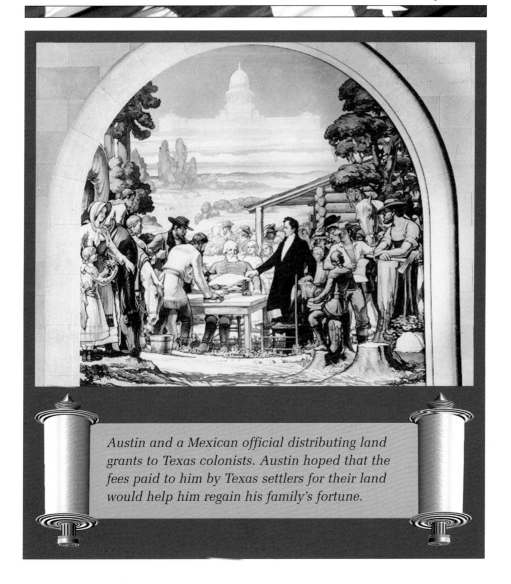

Austin and a Mexican official distributing land grants to Texas colonists. Austin hoped that the fees paid to him by Texas settlers for their land would help him regain his family's fortune.

As time went on, many colonists resented paying Austin's fee of 12½ cents an acre for surveying and other expenses. Word spread that Austin was swindling the settlers out of their hard-earned money. Finally, the griping became so bad that the Mexican authorities canceled the 12½-cent fee and replaced it with a flat $77 charge. That amount barely covered Austin's expenses. He would hardly see any profit. His dream of making a lot of money faded.

Even more serious were charges of favoritism leveled against him. He had a great deal of freedom in how much land he could grant anyone, and he rewarded certain people—those who brought some needed commodity to the colony—with larger grants of land than others. Individuals who performed a service for the colony, such as surveying, were also granted larger parcels of land. People resented that others could get more land than they could, and they grumbled about Austin.

In April 1824, Mexico combined the areas of Texas and neighboring Coahuila into the gigantic state of Coahuila y Texas. While merging Texas with another state diluted its political power and provided no effective government, it did have one benefit: Its capital city of Saltillo was hundreds of miles away, assuring that the Mexican governmental authorities would seldom, if ever, venture into Texas.

Despite the grumbling and his unhappiness at losing some of Texas' political clout, Austin felt confident enough to try to bring his family from Missouri to Texas—but it was not to be. His mother died early in 1824, and his sister Emily, whose husband had died, decided to remarry and stay in Missouri. Austin's friend Joseph Hawkins also died. Feeling very much alone, Austin had just his brother, Brown, for company. In a letter to Emily, Austin morosely described his living conditions as "confusion, dirt, and torment."[3]

In March 1825, a law was passed establishing the empresario system as the official policy of the states. Four other Americans soon received permission to bring settlers to Texas: Robert Leftwich, Haden Edwards, Green DeWitt, and Frost Thorn.

But the expansion of the empresario system carried with it the seeds of its destruction. Not all of them were as conscientious as Austin. For example, after receiving an empresario contract, Haden Edwards tried to make everyone already on his land grant pay him for permission to remain. Edwards was such a bad empresario that the Mexican government canceled his contract in June 1826 and expelled him from Texas. But Edwards did not leave voluntarily, and it took the slow-moving Mexican government several months to organize and deal with him. That gave his brother and his followers time, in December 1826, to revolt and declare Texas the independent

Republic of Fredonia. Although the rebellion was short-lived, it had disastrous long-term consequences for Austin.

Late in 1827, a new constitution for the state of Coahuila y Texas went into effect. The constitution formally made Austin's colony part of the Mexican governmental and legal system, thus relieving him of many of his administrative responsibilities. However, he remained actively involved in political issues that affected his colonists. One issue was slavery. The Mexicans were antislavery, and the government's official position was against slavery. Austin was personally against slavery, but many of his colonists had come to Texas from the American South and brought their slaves with them. Austin knew that they would never accept rules against slavery, so he worked to lessen the effect of Mexican antislavery legislation on his colonists. Laws against slavery would also dry up his flow of settlers from America at exactly the time he was trying to fulfill his additional empresario contracts.

The second issue that he worked on was a law that protected Texas settlers from losing their land or tools for nonpayment of debts in a foreign country. Thus none of those—including Austin—who had left the United States owing money had to worry about losing all they had in Texas.

Texas became known as a shelter for debtors. Sarcastically, they scrawled *GTT* (Gone to Texas) on their front doors as a vague forwarding address for bill collectors and joined the exodus to the state. Although the empresario system was supposed to regulate emigration into Texas, by this time people both good and bad just poured over the border.

After Brown Austin's wedding in the spring of 1828, Stephen began thinking about the possibility of marriage again. His unceasing work for Texas and his colonists had turned him into a careworn, lonely old man—before he was even forty years old. He would have probably liked to find a woman, but as always, Texas took priority over his personal happiness. "Texas is my mistress,"[4] he often said.

Meanwhile, the Fredonian Rebellion had prompted the Mexican congress to fund an expedition to Texas headed by General Manuel de Mier y Terán. Although it was supposed to just survey the United

States–Mexican border, in reality the expedition was to report on conditions in Texas.

Austin and Terán met, and the two developed a mutual respect. However, Austin never realized that Terán had decided that the only way to save Texas for Mexico was to forbid more American immigration into it. Terán found that Americans in Texas, called Texians, outnumbered Tejanos three to one, that their loyalty was questionable, and that many of the Americans entering Texas were not fine families, but dangerous adventurers. "Therefore, I am warning you to take timely measures," Terán reported to the Mexican president. "Texas could throw the whole nation into revolution."[5]

In August 1829, Brown went to New Orleans, caught yellow fever, and died. The news of his beloved brother's death hit Stephen Austin hard. For much of his life he had been plagued by bouts of malaria, and now he was stricken with a severe case. He was in bed for nearly a month, and close to death at times. Although he eventually recovered physically, emotionally he never got over the loss of Brown.

Brown's death affected Stephen's appearance as well. The vigorous, handsome young man of a decade before was long gone. A wrinkled, frail man who seemed to be aging in front of everyone's eyes had replaced him. Consumed by work and tormented by personal grief, he took almost no exercise. On his face was a haunted, gloomy look. Thoughts of personal happiness seemed a lifetime away.

Meanwhile, the volatile course of Mexican politics was about to add to his grief. Another revolution replaced the previous government. On April 6, 1830, the new Mexican government passed a law suspending unfulfilled empresario contracts and prohibiting further American immigration into Texas. In an effort to counterbalance the Americans already there, the government also began forcing Mexicans to move to Texas.

The die had been cast. It was plain to Americans in Texas that the Mexican government viewed them negatively. The Texians now viewed the Mexican government with the same suspicion and alarm with which the Mexicans viewed them.

Austin's dream of Texas as a peaceful Mexican state populated by reputable people was about to evaporate.

The Fredonian Rebellion

The Fredonian Rebellion was a short-lived attempt to gain independence for Texas. However, its long-term effect in making Mexico suspicious of the Texas colonists was devastating.

The story began with Haden Edwards. He received an empresario contract in January 1824 for land near Nacogdoches in northeast Texas. Mexico was eager to populate this area with citizens loyal to them, because in the past Nacogdoches had often been the flashpoint for troubles. Late in 1826, Haden's brother Benjamin and a few other troublemakers drove a small garrison of Mexican troops from Nacogdoches. Then the Edwards brothers and their supporters declared the town to be the capital of the new state of Fredonia, which incorporated most of Texas.

The brothers called for all the other empresarios to support them and appealed for recruits from the United States to help them throw off the yoke of Mexican oppression. They also offered to virtually split Texas with the nearby Native American tribes if they would aid their fight.

The Edwards brothers and their followers had miscalculated. At that time, most Americans in Texas were too content to join any rebellion. In fact, many of the Edwards brothers' own colonists refused to support them. The other empresarios turned their back on them as well. Austin raised a militia force to help Mexican soldiers put down the rebellion.

The rebels had been expecting friends. What they got were enemies. When they saw the forces marshaling against them, the revolt collapsed. By late January 1827, Fredonia was no more.

Austin would point to the Fredonian Rebellion as proof that the empresario system was working: When trouble threatened, the American colonists had come to the aid of Mexico. Mexico saw it differently: Fredonia illustrated the tinderbox that Texas was rapidly becoming. They sent General Terán to Texas to investigate, and his negative report about the situation there ultimately led to the Texas Revolution.

HADEN EDWARDS
EMPRESARIO
LEADER OF THE
FREDONIAN REBELLION, 1826-27
SENT TO THE UNITED STATES
TO RAISE FUNDS FOR
THE TEXAS REVOLUTION, 1836
A LEADER IN THE DEVELOPMENT
OF A NATION
BORN IN VIRGINIA
AUGUST 12, 1771
DIED AUGUST 14, 1849
HIS WIFE
SUSAN BEALL EDWARDS
BORN IN MARYLAND
APRIL 10, 1774
DIED APRIL 6, 1849

For Your Information

Austin shown in an atypical pose, grabbing a rifle at the sound of trouble. In reality, a rifle is probably the last thing Austin would have grabbed.

CHAPTER
5

Revolt!

As soon as he heard about the new law, Austin wrote letters of protest to acting Mexican President Anastacio Bustamante and General Terán, who was now also the general commissioner in charge of colonization affairs in Texas. As the best-known and most respected of all the empresarios, Austin was on friendly terms with both men.

He knew he was heading into dangerous waters. He wanted more freedom for Texas and the various Mexican states, so he befriended politicians with that viewpoint. But the Bustamante government—including Terán—were Centralists. To keep the men as friends, Austin had no choice but to pretend to support their views as well. Supporting both sides could be disastrous if either side found out about his deception.

As Austin straddled the political fence, more Mexican troops were coming into Texas to enforce the April 6 law. Despite the ban on further American settlers, more of them were coming to Texas as well. Many of them were fleeing troubled pasts. "The Sabine River is a greater Savior than Jesus Christ," said one Texas settler, speaking about the river that separated Texas from the United States. "He only saves men when they die from going to Hell but this river saves living men from prison."[1]

Many of the settlers coming into Texas were not the people of good character that Austin and the other empresarios were supposed to seek, but men of volatile temperaments and spotty pasts. Austin, with his conservative, go-along-with-Mexico philosophy, was being viewed more and more as part of the "establishment." These men were seen as the face of the "new" Texas—and the face of the new Texas was finding many things to dislike about Mexico.

In August 1830, Austin was elected as one of two Texas representatives to the state legislature. He was reluctant to attend the legislative sessions, because it would force him to be away from his colonists for a long period of time. He went anyway, mainly to try to prevent the passage of any other laws that would be harmful to his colony. Meanwhile, the Mexican government was collapsing.

After returning to his colony from the state legislature in early June, 1831, Austin had but one thought on his mind: the imminent arrival in Texas of his cousin, Mary Austin Holley. A widow, at forty-seven she looked many years younger. She was a writer and lover of literature, and her intellect was on par with Austin's. Despite the problems that were rumbling through the Texas countryside in the second part of 1831, he allowed himself to focus again on his personal happiness. Perhaps he even imagined a marriage to his smart, beautiful, and fun-loving cousin, and then their retirement to a grand Texas home, where they could spend the rest of their days.

It was not to be. Texas colonists were becoming increasingly belligerent, and General Santa Anna was leading rebel forces against the Bustamante government. Austin was still loyal to the Mexican government, but for the first time he began to think that the only way Texas could ever become the paradise he so desperately wanted it to be was if it became independent from Mexico.

On July 3, 1832, General Terán, leader of the government forces against Santa Anna, committed suicide. Austin knew that the rebels were now very likely to win the war, and he came out in favor of Santa Anna, hoping that the general would grant the reforms that Texas wanted.

By December of that year, there were approximately 15,000 Americans in Texas, and just 3,000 Tejanos. They were fast dividing into the "war" and "peace" parties. Austin, who still favored negotiations, was seen as head of the "peace" party.

On January 3, 1833, Santa Anna entered Mexico City victorious, as Bustamante fled. On March 1, Santa Anna was elected president. On April 1, a convention of Texas delegates—including Sam Houston, the former governor of Tennessee, who had come to Texas late in 1832—met and petitioned the Mexican government for several things, including resumption of American immigration and separate statehood from Coahuila. They also included a constitution for the new state of Texas. They selected Austin to carry the petition to Mexico City.

Austin knew that the request might generate problems; the new constitution, echoing the American constitution, was like a trumpet announcing Texas's desire for separation from Mexico. However, he was trapped. His standing among the Americans in Texas was sinking; his cautious, pro-government policy had lost favor among the colonists and made many view him with suspicion. As one man wrote: "Col. Austin's sincerity in this matter [separate statehood for Texas] is much doubted by many people in Texas."[2] Austin was proud of his reputation among the Texas settlers; he *had* to go to show that he was still their leader.

Before he left San Felipe in April 1833 for Mexico City, Austin wrote a forlorn letter to Mary Austin Holley. He realized that his dream of retiring to a peaceful life on a farm free from politics—and perhaps with her—was just that: a dream. Texas politics had captured him and would never let him go. He told her that he was "farther from all hopes of farm and home than I ever was."[3]

Austin arrived in Mexico City on July 18, after a rough sea voyage and a grueling overland trip. Virtually every Mexican official he met along the way informed him that the April 1 convention of settlers was illegal; under Mexican law, nobody but the state legislatures could petition for statehood. Worse yet, a cholera epidemic was killing thousands. Austin also got reports of cholera raging unchecked in Texas.

In a worried, depressed state, frustrated by the snail's pace of political events, Austin on October 2 wrote a letter to the San Antonio *ayuntamiento* (local ruling council) that urged Texians to organize a government independent of Coahuila. A few weeks later, in a meeting with Vice President Valentín Gómez Farías, Austin told him: "Texas must be made a state by the Govt. or she would make herself one."[4]

Despite those revolutionary sentiments, Austin was pleased when he left Mexico City on December 10. Santa Anna seemed sympathetic to Texas, and he agreed to repeal the restriction on American immigration. Things seemed to be going well.

That's why Austin was stunned when he was arrested on January 3, 1834.

The problem was his October 2 letter advocating independence without waiting for the federal government's approval. The *ayuntamiento* had sent it to the governor of Texas y Coahuila, who was not pleased. Alternately, some historians say that the letter found its way back to Mexico City and Santa Anna. Either way, the letter was a call for revolution and sealed Austin's fate.

Although he was moved to several different prisons, and the conditions of his captivity were relaxed so that he was permitted books and socialization, Austin remained in jail until December 1834. Finally, on Christmas Day, he was released on bail. He had been imprisoned almost one year.

Under his bail terms, Austin had to remain in Mexico City. Thus he was in a perfect position to watch the next act in the Mexican government's struggle. Santa Anna had only pretended to be a liberal supporter of states' rights. Instead, in the spring of 1835, he quickly moved to become a dictator. He abolished congress and dissolved all state legislatures and even the states themselves, turning them into powerless departments in a central government with himself as ruler. Instead of independent, Texas became insignificant.

Zacatecas, another Mexican state that had pressed for greater independence, resisted Santa Anna's actions. In response, Santa Anna's army roared through the capital city of Zacatecas, destroying it. The message to Texas was clear.

Austin, however, was preoccupied with his own affairs. At the end of June 1835, as part of a general amnesty law, he was finally allowed to leave Mexico City. He arrived in New Orleans by ship in early August 1835, then sailed for Texas.

However, his long imprisonment and impatience with the constantly changing Mexican political situation seems to have finally taken their toll on him. In his first communication with Mary Austin Holley in two years, he argued that Texas should become part of the United States. He called Santa Anna "a base, unprincipled bloody monster."[5] Perhaps understandably, his concern for Mexico had vanished. He urged Holley to write in support of encouraging as much American emigration to Texas as possible, to push forward the day when Texas would become part of the United States.

On September 8, Austin arrived in Texas to a hero's welcome. Both sides in Texas—war and peace—welcomed him. He was elected chairman of the newly formed Committee of Correspondence and Vigilance.

By this time, settlers were swarming into Texas, most of them spoiling for a fight. This new version of the American Revolution had many willing participants. Military men not only from the United States but also from other countries were streaming into Texas.

Austin had to move quickly. Because of the rebellious atmosphere, Mexican General Martín Perfect de Cos, Santa Anna's brother-in-law, was heading to Texas with troops to disarm the colonists and make arrests.

Cos sent a column of troops to the Texas town of Gonzalez to arrest agitators and reclaim a small cannon the Mexicans had given the Texians. The Texians, under a banner reading "Come and Take It," forced the Mexicans to retreat at gunpoint. The revolution had begun.

Cos occupied San Antonio. Austin, although his health had become so poor that he had to be helped onto his horse, headed for Gonzalez in early October, 1835. There, an "Army of the People" of Texas volunteers had assembled and was ready to head to San Antonio. Although his military experience was very limited, Austin was elected commander in chief. Even so, he continually encountered resistance and sometimes outright refusal from his fiercely independent army commanders to follow orders.

Finally, on November 12, 1835, perhaps realizing that diplomacy, not fighting, was Austin's strength, the provisional Texas government voted to send him to the United States to drum up support for Texas. As Sam Houston said, "his identity . . . would have more influence in [Texas's] behalf than all men in Texas united."[6]

It must have bothered Austin to be absent from Texas just as the real fighting seemed about to start, but his beloved Texas needed him, so off he went.

Austin's trip to America lasted six months, from January to June. His list of tasks was long: negotiate a million-dollar loan, buy weapons for the army and ships for a navy, receive donations, and get people excited about the Texas cause so that they would come down and fight. Thus Austin was away when the gloomy news arrived about Santa Anna's massacre of Texas volunteers at the Alamo on March 6, 1836, and his seemingly unstoppable march through Texas. "My heart and soul are sick but my spirit is unbroken,"[7] he said.

Then, on April 21, the Texas army under Sam Houston routed the Mexicans at the Battle of San Jacinto, and also captured Santa Anna. Texas's independence had been won. It was now a republic—a completely sovereign nation. Austin knew he must return immediately.

At the Battle of San Jacinto in April 1836, a Texian army under Sam Houston caught the Mexican army under Santa Anna unawares, and won a smashing victory that guaranteed Texas's independence. The battle lasted less than 30 minutes, and Texian casualties were slight.

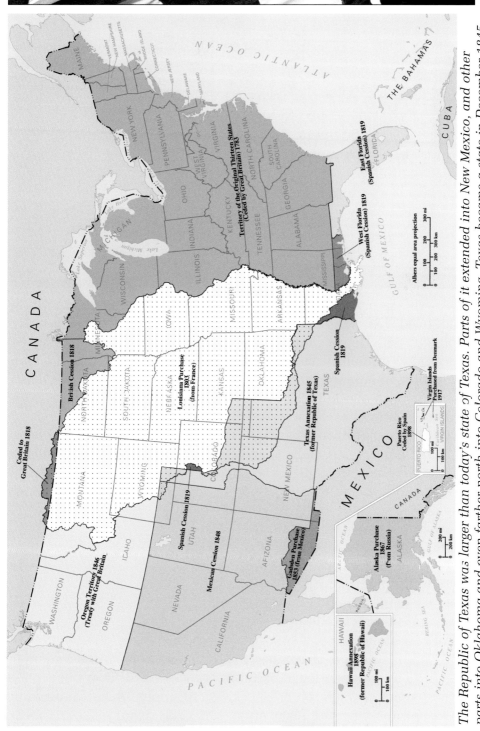

The Republic of Texas was larger than today's state of Texas. Parts of it extended into New Mexico, and other parts into Oklahoma and even farther north into Colorado and Wyoming. Texas became a state in December 1845.

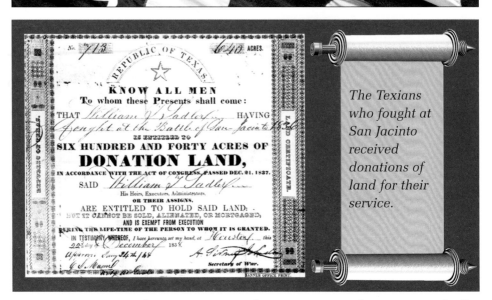

The Texians who fought at San Jacinto received donations of land for their service.

Austin returned to Texas in late June. Within a month he announced his candidacy for the post of Texas President. His opponent was Henry Smith of the provisional government. Austin appeared confident of victory. But just eleven days before the election, Houston entered the race. Austin knew that he had no chance against the popular hero, and he was right. On election day, Houston received 5,119 votes, Austin just 587.

By then Austin was likely too ill to care. Another attack of fever, probably malaria, struck him, and he spent the rest of September in bed. He coughed constantly, and his face was lined and worn. But he rallied, and felt well enough to accept an appointment as Houston's secretary of state.

Austin traveled to Columbia, Texas, a tiny town that was the capital city of the new republic. He rented a small room with no fireplace or stove; it became both his bedroom and office.

A winter storm hit Columbia at the end of December. Austin caught a cold, which turned into pneumonia. His condition worsened, and there was little the doctors could do as he slipped in and out of consciousness.

Around noon on December 27, 1836, Austin awoke and murmured, "The independence of Texas is recognized! Don't you see it in the papers?"[8] Then he fell back, unconscious. A half hour later, the forty-three-year-old Texas empresario was dead.

Sam Houston

Along with Stephen Austin, Sam Houston (right) is one of the most important figures in the early history of Texas. However, because Austin died just after Texas won its independence, Houston usually overshadows Austin.

Houston was born on March 2, 1793, near Lexington, Virginia. When his father died in 1807, his mother moved the family to eastern Tennessee. There, Houston spent several years living with the Cherokee, learning their language and customs.

After serving under Andrew Jackson in the War of 1812, Houston studied law and was elected the district attorney of Nashville, Tennessee. He then served two terms in Congress, and was elected governor of Tennessee in 1827.

Two years later, Houston, charged with infidelity and alcoholism, separated from his wife Eliza and went back to live with the Cherokee. Reportedly he drank so much with them that they called him "big drunk." He also had a Cherokee wife.

By 1835 he was living part-time in the Texas town of Nacogdoches near the border with Louisiana. When rebellion broke out against Mexico, Houston was made commander of the Texas Army. He kept retreating against the superior forces of Santa Anna until April 21, 1836, when he launched a surprise attack at San Jacinto. His overwhelming victory there guaranteed Texas's independence.

Houston was elected the first president of the newly independent Republic of Texas. After Texas became an American state, Houston was elected as one of its first senators. However, as civil war loomed, he opposed secession from the Union, a view that made him unpopular. Nevertheless, he was elected governor in 1859. Because he refused to swear allegiance to the Confederacy, he was removed from office in 1861. He died two years later, on July 26, 1863.

Chronology

1793	Stephen Fuller Austin is born in Austinville, Virginia, to Moses and Maria Austin.
c. 1795	His sister Emily is born.
1798	Stephen and his family move to Missouri.
1803	His brother, James Elijah Brown, is born.
1804	Stephen attends Bacon Academy in Connecticut.
1807	He graduates from Bacon Academy and enrolls in Transylvania University in Lexington, Kentucky.
1810	He leaves Transylvania University to help his father in his mining business.
1812	Stephen takes a disastrous barge trip down the Mississippi River to New Orleans.
1813	He becomes an ensign in Missouri militia.
1815	He wins election to Missouri legislature.
1816	He leases the mines from his father.
1819	Stephen goes to Long Prairie, in what is today southwestern Arkansas, to make a fortune on land claims. His enterprise fails.
1821	Moses Austin receives a land grant to settle 300 families in Texas. He dies before he can go. Stephen goes to Texas and assumes his father's land grant there.
1822	Stephen arrives in Mexico to regain authority to distribute land in Texas.
1823	The Texas colonization request is approved; Austin becomes the first Texas empresario.
1824	His mother dies; San Felipe de Austin is established in Stephen's honor.
1826	Haden Edwards and his brothers stage the Fredonian Rebellion to gain Texas independence; Austin helps the Mexican troops put down the rebellion.
1829	Stephen's brother, Brown, dies.
1830	Mexico cancels empresario contracts. In August, Austin is elected as one of two Texas representatives to the state legislature.
1833	Santa Anna overthrows Mexican government. Austin goes to Mexico to argue for the empresario contracts.
1834	He is arrested on January 3 and imprisoned in Mexico; he is released on December 25.
1835	Austin returns to Texas on September 8; he commands Texas forces but is reassigned as diplomat.
1836	In January, he goes to the United States to drum up support for Texas independence. After Sam Houston defeats Santa Anna, Austin returns to Republic of Texas. He dies in Columbia, Texas, on December 27.

Timeline in History

1775	American Revolution starts with the battles of Lexington and Concord.
1776	Declaration of Independence is issued.
1781	Cornwallis surrenders to Washington at Yorktown.
1789	The French Revolution begins.
1796	George Washington gives his farewell address.
1803	Thomas Jefferson completes the Louisiana Purchase, which doubles the size of the United States.
1811	The New Madrid earthquakes begin.
1812	War of 1812 is declared.
1815	Napoleon Bonaparte is defeated at Waterloo.
1819	The United States gives up all claims to Texas in a treaty with Spain, which gives Florida to the United States.
1821	The first American colonists go to Texas.
1828	The border between the United States and Mexico is set at the Sabine River. Noah Webster writes the *American Dictionary of the English Language*.
1835	The Texas freedom fighters defend a small brass cannon at the Gonzales settlement against Mexican soldiers who have come to reclaim it, beginning the Texas Revolution.
1836	Texas declares independence from Mexico; the Alamo falls to Santa Anna in March; in April, Battle of San Jacinto results in an overwhelming victory for Texas and therefore Texas independence.
1837	Samuel Morse invents the telegraph.
1845	President John Tyler signs a congressional joint resolution annexing Texas to the United States. Mexico breaks off diplomatic relations with the United States in anger over the Texas annexation.
1846	The Mexican War begins; it ends in 1848 with the United States victorious over Mexico.
1861	The American Civil War begins. Texas joins the Confederate States of America.
1863	Sam Houston dies. Thanksgiving Day is declared an official holiday.
1865	The Civil War ends.
1871	The Great Chicago Fire kills 300 people.
1876	Alexander Graham Bell patents the telephone.
1879	Thomas Edison discovers a filament material for his electric lightbulb.
1881	Billy the Kid is killed in New Mexico.
1883	Texas purchases the Alamo to preserve it as a historic shrine.
1886	The Statue of Liberty is dedicated.

Chapter Notes

Chapter One. Imprisoned

1. Gregg Cantrell, *Stephen F. Austin—Empresario of Texas* (New Haven, Connecticut: Yale University Press, 1999), p. 295.

Chapter Two. Early Life

1. Gregg Cantrell, *Stephen F. Austin—Empresario of Texas* (New Haven, Connecticut: Yale University Press, 1999), p. 62.

Chapter Three. Gone to Texas

1. Time-Life Books, Inc., *The Texans* (New York: Time-Life Books, 1975), p. 16.

2. Ibid., p. 24.

3. Gregg Cantrell, *Stephen F. Austin—Empresario of Texas* (New Haven, Connecticut: Yale University Press, 1999), p. 88.

4. James L. Haley, *Texas—An Album of History* (Garden City, New York: Doubleday & Company Inc., 1985), p. 16.

Chapter Four. The Empresario

1. Gregg Cantrell, *Stephen F. Austin—Empresario of Texas*

(New Haven, Connecticut: Yale University Press, 1999), p. 125.

2. James L. Haley, *Texas—An Album of History* (Garden City, New York: Doubleday & Company Inc., 1985), p. 19.

3. Cantrell, p. 167.

4. John Hoyt Williams, *Sam Houston* (New York: Simon & Schuster, 1993), p. 103.

5. Haley, p. 24.

Chapter Five. Revolt!

1. John Hoyt Williams, *Sam Houston* (New York: Simon & Schuster, 1993), p. 108.

2. Gregg Cantrell, *Stephen F. Austin—Empresario of Texas* (New Haven, Connecticut: Yale University Press, 1999), p. 264.

3. Ibid., p. 266.

4. Ibid., p. 273.

5. James L. Haley, *Texas—An Album of History* (Garden City, New York: Doubleday & Company Inc., 1985), p. 33.

6. Williams, p. 127.

7. Cantrell, p. 345.

8. Ibid., p. 364.

Further Reading

Books

Adams, Simon, and David Murdoch. *Texas*. New York: DK Publishing, 2003.

Garland, Sherry. *A Line in the Sand: The Alamo Diary of Lucinda Lawrence, Gonzales, Texas, 1835*. New York: Scholastic, 1998.

Haley, James L. *Stephen F. Austin and the Founding of Texas*. New York: PowerPlus Books, 2003.

Murphy, Jim. *Inside the Alamo*. New York: Delacorte Press, 2003.

Nardo, Don. *The Mexican-American War*. San Diego: Lucent Books, 1999.

Stanley, Jerry. *Cowboys & Longhorns*. New York: Crown Publishers, 2003.

Works Consulted

Cantrell, Gregg. *Stephen F. Austin—Empresario of Texas*. New Haven, Connecticut: Yale University Press, 1999.

Fehrenbach, T.R. *Lone Star*. New York: The Macmillan Company, 1968.

Frantz, Joe B. *Texas—A Bicentennial History*. New York: W.W. Norton & Company, Inc., 1976.

Haley, James L. *Texas—An Album of History*. Garden City, New York: Doubleday & Company Inc., 1985.

Time-Life Books, Inc. *The Texans*. New York: Time-Life Books, 1975.

Williams, John Hoyt. *Sam Houston*. New York: Simon & Schuster, 1993.

On the Internet

The Alamo
http://www.thealamo.org

Barker, Eugene C., and James W. Pohl. "Texas Revolution" http://www.tsha.utexas.edu/handbook/online/articles/view/TT/qdt1.html

Famous Texans: Sam Houston http://www.famoustexans.com/samhouston.htm

Handbook of Texas Online: Austin, Stephen Fuller. http://www.tsha.utexas.edu/handbook/online/articles/AA/fau14.html

Sons of Dewitt Colony, Texas: Antonio López de Santa Anna http://www.tamu.edu/ccbn/dewitt/santaanna.htm

Texas Beyond History http://www.texasbeyondhistory.net/

Index